GOSPEL POEMS

BY

DONAL HILL

Dedication

This book is dedicated to Preacher Scott W. Hickey. He never gave up on me. When Donal was about 12 years old, he would cross paths with Scott Hickey. Scott would be walking the road to his church at the time, called Oak Grove Baptist Church, and I was going the opposite direction. That invitation from Scott W Hickey the night I got my new bike with a new horn and light was one I will never forget. "I was saved!" Later, the church merged with Pleasant Grove Church off HWY 277 in Anson, Texas. The sign to the church still shines bright!

Acknowledgements

My grandmother and grandfather, who raised me after my mom passed away. I would stay with them after school and on weekends, along with my father!

I would also like to thank everyone for their prayers for this book!

Author Biography

Donal Hill is a good o' country boy born in Anson, Texas, on the 23rd day of June 1935, to the proud parents of Frank and Annie Hill.

Donal had 8 other brothers and sisters and unfortunately one passed away a few months after birth. His mother passed away when he was only 2 years old. But, his grandparents raised him after along with his father. Donal did not remember much about his mother but remembers being outdoors hunting and fishing.

When Donal bought his first bike, it had a light and a horn. Preacher, Scott W. Hickey, invited Donal and his friend to his church Revival that very night. That night he turned his bike light on and rode for 3 miles with his friend. Donal's light shined on Jesus that night and that was just the beginning.

Donal graduated from Hawley High School and later had four handsome sons. Three of them passed away with cancer and one son died in a car accident. He has a beautiful intelligent daughter who gave him two granddaughters and he also has two grandsons.

Thirty years ago, Donal was blessed and owned and operated HillCo Drywall in Buda, Texas. His daughter has been running the office for about a year now. Donal experienced life to its fullest or so he thought - consisting of money, philandering and gambling.

In April 2022, at the age of 86, the Lord spoke to Donal creating these easy-to-read Gospel Poems, which are inspired from the Bible. "Simple yet not changing any of it", Donal stated. "Put Jesus in between you and the devil. Open your heart and let the Lord in!"

Table of Contents

Adam and Eve

God planted the earth - with herbs, grass and trees.

Was no one there - to take care of His needs.

Formed man of the dust - In his nostrils did breathe.

Became a living soul - to take care of His needs.

That's how man was formed - from the dust of the earth.

Dust was God's formula - to create man's birth.

Planted trees in the garden - for you and me.

To produce fruit - for us don't you see?

One tree He planted - Said, "Don't eat this." Here's why.

"If you eat it - you will surely die."

God saw Adam - Said, "This is not fate,

I need to give you - a help mate."

He put him to sleep – took one of his ribs.

He made woman - His help mate to give.

They were both naked - Did not know,

That they were exposed - and needed clothes.

Adam named Eve - Known throughout the land.

Names her woman - she was made from man.

The serpent told Eve - "Eat of the tree.

Make you smart as God - That's how you will be."

She looked at the fruit - and she did eat.

Gave some to her husband - said - "Here, have a treat."

They both did eat - Then they did know.

They both were naked – Used fig leaves for clothes.

Lord came in the garden – Called out their names.

They were hid cause they were so ashamed.

After all this happened – This is when.

The first sin on earth - did just begin.

1

Baptized

John Baptized Jesus - for all the world to see.
Setting the example - there for you and me.
We are baptized with water - this is not the most.
Jesus will baptize you - with the Holy Ghost.

Jesus did not baptize - His disciples did it for Him.
Now days the preachers - will baptize them.
You are baptized - for the remission of sins.
Receive the Holy Ghost - Seals everything then.

Anytime there's water - that will be fine.
You can be baptized - at any time.
When you go under - washes away old sins.
When you come up - you're revived again.

Baptized in the name of Jesus - no other way.
In Jesus' name - is the only way.
Not matter what - is your nationality.
All are one body - when baptized you see.

Birthday

Stop hold everything - it's time to celebrate.

It's Jesus Birthday - Hurry don't be late.

I don't know how old he is - He's been gone a while.

If he appears - He will surely be in Stiles.

He will probably come in spirit - The time is not yet given.

For him to claim us as his own - and take us all to heaven.

To go on his heavenly party - You'll really be excited.

Except him as your Savior - So you will be invited!

Ask him to save you - That's all you do.

He will come in your heart - and instantly save you.

Let's check out the party - See what's going on.

Maybe their a present - To decorate your throne.

I see presents everywhere - As I check them through.

I've looked and I've looked - There's no present for you.

How could they overlook - Such a dear, dear friend.

Just like on the cross - rejected once again.

Jesus, I thank you so much - That you are so forgiving.

That you would overlook our wrong -Still take us to heaven.

Compare Your Heart Like it is a Door

Compare your heart like it's a door – No door knob outside.

Only way to open it – is you from the inside.

Means you are the only way – for someone to come in.

So when God knocks on the door – Will you let him in.

We know your heart is full of sin – Also filled with Strife.

Except him as your savior – And receive eternal life.

Confess with your mouth – and Believe in your heart.

That God raised him from the dead – You want him in your heart.

For with the heart man believe – with the mouth confession made.

Except him as your Savior – And be saved today.

He died upon the cross – Just for you and me.

It cost you nothing - cause your salvations is free.

Thank you so much Jesus – For providing us a way.

For us to go to heaven – and with you always stay.

Convert another Sinner Hides a Multitude of Sin

Living without sinning is so very hard to do.

I can think of only one - and He gave His life for you.

To me there's two kinds of people - living on this earth

There're lost sinners and saved sinners - which receiveth second birth.

After Jesus saves you - you'll want to go His way.

But the devil's always after you - each and every day.

The best way you can fight him - and know you're gonna win

Is convert another sinner - It hides a multitude of sin.

God said He'd give you power - through the Holy Ghost.

That we may witness for Him - to all parts of the earth.

So lay not treasures on this earth - where thieves break in and steal.

Put your treasures in heaven - It's the perfect deal.

When you feel God's spirit - it touches deep within.

You can't see His spirit - neither can you see the wind.

If you fall short on things above - but you still want to win.

Just convert another sinner - It hides a multitude of sin.

The first thing you let them know - is God says All have sinned

But their hearts may be cleansed - if they let the master in.

The wages you get from sin is a horrible reward.

But the gift of God is eternal life - through Jesus Christ our Lord.

Ask them to confess with their mouth - the Lord Jesus Christ.

And believe God raised Him from the dead - and they'll have eternal life.

So please don't be ashamed - if a soul you want to win.

Just convert another sinner - It hides a multitude of sin.

David Fights Goliath

Goliath the Philistine - was a giant of a man.
About ten feet tall - with very large hands.
The people of Israel – he hoped soon would fall.
Fighting one on one - and the winner take all.
With a helmet of brass - upon his head,
Four-hundred-pound coat - heavy as lead.
Shoulders and legs - shielded with brass.
A fifty-pound spear - he threw very fast.

He challenged again - Said, "If you kill me,
The Philistine people - your servants will be.
If I kill your man - make sure there's no fuss.
Israelite people - will surely serve us."
Saul heard his challenge - dismayed and afraid.
"The man that kills Goliath - shall surely be paid."
The men were scared - and stayed far away.
None was a match - for this giant today.

Jesse's young son - tended the sheep.
His brothers in battle - in this valley deep.
Jesse told David - "Take them food to eat."
He left a keeper - to tend the sheep.
David, the youth - had a ruddy decent.
Went to the battle - where they pitched their tent.

Goliath challenged again - David's temper did prod.
"Defying the armies - of our living God!"
His brothers heard - what David had said.

Was kinda embarrassed - Their faces turned red.
David was serious -Spare not the rod.
"I slay this giant - for our living God."

King Saul got the message - He surely did.
He saw David - "You're only a kid!"
Saul told David - "You can't fight this man.
He's well trained - at protecting the land."

"The lion and the bear - took a lamb and ran.
I grabbed them by the beard -slew them with my hands.
I killed them both - spared not the rod.
I'll slay this Philistine - for defying our God."
David put on his armor – could hardly move.
Spoke to Saul said - "This isn't cool."
He told Saul - "This I can't use.
Give me my sling - and five rocks that are smooth."

Goliath cursed David - as they did meet.
Said, "The fowls of the air - your body will eat!"
David said "I come - not with spear or shield.
In the name of God - you, I will kill."

Took a stone from his bag - and quickly flung it.
It struck in his forehead - a perfect hit.
The giant hit the ground – He wasn't quite dead.
David grabbed the giant's sword - and cut off his head.
David went to Saul - with the head in his hand.
This kid was braver - than all other men.
All Israel was proud - Praise him they did.
It was so amazing - The faith of the kid!

Deep Within

He gave His life - on Calvary's tree.
He shed His blood - just for you and me.
He's my Savior - my Lord and my friend.
So let ole' Satan perish - cause my Lord is deep within,
Deep within - deep within.
So let ole' Satan perish - cause my Lord is deep within.

Oh, the places - that I have been.
But he forgave me - of each and every sin.
He's my Savior - my Lord and my friend.
So let ole' Satan perish - cause my Lord is deep within,
Deep within - deep within.
So let ole' Satan perish - cause my Lord is deep within.

If you will ask him - your sins He will mend.
Then you'll have that blessing - of Jesus deep within.
He's my Savior -my Lord and my friend.
So let ole' Satan perish - cause my Lord is deep within,
Deep within - deep within.
So let ole' Satan perish cause - my Lord is deep within.

Depart From Me

When you worship Jesus - Do it from your Heart
So, when it's your judgment time – He won't say, "depart".
Anything to do with God – Build it on a Rock.
When Satan tries to interfere - he's already blocked.
You say, "I cast out devils" - For all the world to see.
Did I do it for God - Or do it for me?
Don't try to fool Jesus - He knows your heart, you see.
Don't try to fool him - with your inequity.
With a loving heart - always to him, be true.
Always try to serve him - in everything you do.
The worst you could hear God say - When comes back for you,
Depart from me sinner- I never knew you.

Divorce

Letter of divorcement - Is what we're speaking of, "Is it alright with the master up above?"

Except for fornication – all is NOT well.

You are taking a chance - of going to hell.

The one you are divorcing, "is committing adultery".

This is NOT good with Jesus - don't you see.

Adultery is very easy - for you to commit.

Look at her in lust - and you are doing it.

Keep your eyes in control - Be careful what you do.

With your mind in control - so he will be proud of you.

Be sure when you marry - it is NOT for lust.

But for the one you really love and trust.

Esther

Ahasuerus the King - asked Queen Vashti to come.

But she wouldn't - She was really dumb.

Made him very mad - Here's what I'll do.

Get me another queen - to take the place of you.

The King appointed officers - This is where they went.

Searching for this virgin - in every providence.

They searched everywhere - till all of them were seen.

For the perfect virgin - to satisfy the King.

Many, many girls were there - on display.

Except the girl named Ester - She was hid away.

Mordecai kept her hidden - She would not be seen.

Before he was - ready for her to meet the King.

Esther was taken to the King - on the seventh year.

When the King saw her - Wanted to keep her near.

The King loved Ester more - than any virgin shown.

Made her his Queen - and put her on his throne.

Every Eye Shall See – Every Tongue Confess

Every eye shall see – every tongue confess.

When Jesus comes again – Won't be any rest.

Do you think you're ready – When He come back again?

It will be very sad – For a lot of our friends.

Think what you are doing – So the judgement won't be bad.

Then when the judgment comes – You'll be very glad.

He might come again – as a thief in the night.

Be sure you are ready – So all will be alright.

Every eye shall see – and every tongue confess.

Thank you so much Jesus – For giving us the best.

The Lord is coming soon – and ready I will be.

I'm gonna claim the mansion – that he made for me.

Faith

Faith can cast the mountains - in the sea.

Faith can heal the sick - if they believe.

Faith can take the fearfulness away.

Faith becomes stronger - when you pray.

Faith can make the blind to see.

Faith is a gift for you and me.

Faith and make the lame to walk,

Faith can make the dumb to talk,

Faith can make the demons flee.

Faith can remove the sycamore tree.

Faith can make old Satan flee.

Faith is the hope, for you and me.

There's no one on this globe,

That has the faith he gave Job.

Be not like waves that are tossed about.

Be strong in Jesus, without a doubt

First Last or Last First

First last or last first? That's what the bible says.

Where will you be classified - When your score is read.

Will you be number one or way on down the line.

When the lord says-It's your judgment time.

It's time to prepare yourself -So you will pass the test.

So your grade is high- Will be your very best.

Read your bible study hard - So you'll know what to do.

Then, Jesus will be- very proud of you.

That will be very good- when Jesus comes again.

Then, he will tell you - very good my friend.

Now you have prepared yourself -Don't worry anymore.

You may be first in line - To reach the heavens door!

Fishers of Men

I really like to fish - I always have fun.
Sometimes I don't catch any - Sometimes only one.
Sometimes we catch a bunch - Sometimes only two.
If I throw them back - what good did it do?
I spent a lot of time - and spent a lot on gas.
A lot of times was wasted -Next time I might pass.

Let's try something else - Think of this, my friend.
Tell someone of Jesus - Be a fisher of men.
I told someone of Jesus - He accepted Him right then.
Now I guess you could say - "I'm a fisher of men."
The reward is very great - when a soul you win.
So come on and join me - Be a fisher of men.

When you get to heaven - and Jesus calls your friend,
Tells you "Thank You" - For being my fisher of men.
I didn't need a rod - Didn't need a reel.
Just told them of Jesus -He's the real deal!

Front Row Seat

Mary Magdalene, Joanna - and the mother of James
Went to the sepulcher - It wasn't the same.
Early in the morning - first day of the week.
These three people - had a front row seat.
They entered the sepulcher - A young man in white
Said, "Jesus has risen" - There was much fright.
Tell the disciples and Peter - what you should do.
Go into Galilee - There He'll see you.
They went out quickly - trembling and amazed.
Said nothing to no man - They were so afraid.
Seven devils had been cast - from Mary Magdalene.
After Jesus arose - she was the first on the scene.
There was mourning and weeping - She told on the spot,
That Jesus had risen - They believed her not.
Two walking in the country - and He appeared to them.
They told the residence - did not believe Him.
Appeared to the eleven - as they sat at meat.
Thomas was missing - there's one vacant seat.
He said - Preach the gospel - be baptized and saved.
At your time of death-overcome your grave.
Those that believe- here's the prize you've won.
You can cast out devils - and speak in new tongues.
Drink deadly things-- Won't hurt you bother.
Lay your hands on the sick - and they shall recover.
After He had spoken - He disappeared like a fog.
Went on to heaven at the right hand of God.
They all went forth - and preached everywhere.
Lord, working through signs - As he heard their prayer.
Are you a doubter like Thomas - Feel the prints in his hands.
Thrust your hand in His side - like a real he man.
You know what you missed - would really be neat?
Be with Mary and the others - on that front row seat!

Good Intentions

Tonight as I lay sleeping -"I heard the trumpet sound."

Light came down from Heaven - Lighting everything around!

The Lord has come to claim his own - He came for you and me.

The price he paid upon the cross - to set us captives free.

I forgot to say my prayers - Bible not read in days.

He caught me at a bad time - What will the master say?

If I knew he was coming - on this very night.

I planned to be ready - Did Satan win this fight?

I was driving down the freeway - Someone pulled in front of me.

I let a bad word slip - should have let it be.

I thought to myself - I need to change my way.

I planned to go to church - but I didn't go today.

This friend that was lost - I saw him just today.

We talked and joked around - Then, he went away.

He will go straight to hell - because he does NOT know.

I planned to tell of Jesus - to hell he'll surely go.

The other day we went out - was just after work.

We had a drink or two - I was a total jerk.

There will always be a stumbling block - Satan will see to that.

I'll surely speak of Jesus - the next time we are out.

The weather was very cold - close to zero.

Need to check my neighbor - he is very old.

Then, something else came up - So, I did NOT go.

My intentions were good - that did NOT help you know.

He Goes to Prepare a Place

Praise Him, Praise Him - That's how I plead my case.

While He's up in heaven - preparing us a place.

Love is the word - that we should discuss.

He loves us so much - He's doing this for us.

During His creation -six days - He did work.

While preparing everything - down here on this earth.

He said, "I will go -and prepare a place for you.

Will come again to claim you -That's what He said - "I'll do."

"I will pave the streets with gold - flowers everywhere.

Think of all the beauty - I made for you to share."

Wind is like the spirit - can feel but you can't see.

Heaven is a spirit -for those that will believe.

Lift up the gates of your mind - Let Jesus fill the void.

Cause anytime He's involved - it will not come back void.

Cloud that took Jesus away - will return again the same.

Be ready for His return - so He will call your name.

Your mind serves God - your flesh serves sin.

Be sure your mind is working - when Jesus comes again.

To live is Christ - and to die is gain.

Trading this old sinful earth - for our heavenly domain.

Every knee shall bow - every tongue confess.

Be sure you have this done - before you face the test.

However you are - you should be content.

Let him guide you day by day - He'll always be your friend.

All shall know the Lord - from the least to the greatest.

Be sure you are prepared - so your greatest is your latest.

Hi Mom

I don't remember Mama - She died when I was two.
God needed her in heaven - had some things for her to do.
She went on to serve Him -Left us down here below.
I'd like to see my mama - They said she loved me so.
Dad said when she was sick - and couldn't get around,
She'd lie there in her bed - with a mirror in her hand.
She'd hold the mirror watching me - at least that's what I'm told.
I haven't seen my mama - since I was two years old.

The quarterback on the football team - just threw a long bomb!
The camera flashed upon his face- His lips said, "Hi Mom."
Cold chills ran down my spine - Wish I could do the same.
As I'm sitting in my living room - watching this football game.
People just don't know - how to appreciate their mom.
They take her for granted - That is pretty dumb.
You never know how long she'll live - Then she'll be gone.
Show her that you love her - before God calls her home.
When my life on earth is over - and I am heaven bound,
I'm gonna see my mama -You can bet your boots I am.
Get my mansion ready - cause Lord, here I come.
As I step through those pearly gates - I'll get to say, "Hi Mom."

In The Beginning

In the beginning - there were no births.

Then, God created - heavens and earth.

He created the earth - that was no bother.

Created the earth - on the face of the water.

Let there be light - I knew he could.

Separated from darkness - and it was good.

Called the darkness, night. The light he called, day.

And the evening and the morning - was the first day.

Divided the water - in his own way.

Called the firmament heaven - was the second day.

The land he called, earth - The waters he called, seas.

He did all of this - for you and for me.

On the earth - he had a plan.

All kinds of seeds - throughout the land.

There was grass, herbs - and all the fruits, he could.

He looked upon it - said that it's really good.

Let me tell you something - here's what I'll say.

All this happened - was on the third day.

Then God said, Let there be light!"

To divide the day - from the night.

Made the sun, moon - and also made the stars.

To light up the earth - so we can see, afar.

Sun was by day - moon, and stars by night.

To light up everything - such a pretty sight.

God said, "It was good" - That's what I say.

And the evening and the morning - was the fourth day.

Let the waters bring fourth - every fish in the sea.

And the fowls fill the air. All the birds to see.
Be fruitful and multiply - that's how it shall be.
All the birds in the air - and the fish in the sea.
His creations - are still underway.
The morning and the evening - was the fifth day.
God made the best - and the cattle to roam the fields.
Made man and woman to rule them - this was his will.
Man made in his image - then made him a mate.
To rule over all - this was really great.
Gave you every herd - every fowl in the air.
For the food you will need - just have to prepare.
He looked around - like we knew he would.
Said, "I'm pleased - Everything is good!"
Everything is complete - this I will say.
And the evening and the morning - was the sixth day.

Israelites Out of Egypt

By the mountain of God – Moses tended the flock

He was so surprised – Really got a shock

The bush there by him – Burst into flame

It was not consumed – Remaining the same

God spoke from the bush – Said "Look around,"

"Remove your shoes, Moses – You're on hallowed ground.

God told Moses – "Do this for me

Go tell Pharoah – To set my people free."

Moses was scared – Didn't know what to do

God said, "Don't worry, - I'll be there with you."

What will the children – Of Israel say to me?

Why are you here – Here to set you free.

Well, who sent you – I'll tell them I am

God said "I am that I am."

You was (were) mistreated – Didn't have much money

God's bringing you to a land – Flowing with Milk and honey.

Now the king of Egypt – Won't let you go

God will smite him – Change his mind, don't you know.

Moses said, "Lord – They won't believe me.

That you have sent me – To set them free."

Is that a good rod in your hand? – Moses said "Yes, it isn't fake."

"Then cast it on the ground" – And it turned into a snake.

Moses was scared – Afraid it would bite his bod.

Picked it up by the tail – Turned back to a rod.

Put your hand in your tummy - Then you will see.

He was so scared – Turned into leprosy.

Put his hand there again – Let out with a cheer

When he took it out – It was completely clear.

Took water from the river – That was about to flood
Put it on the ground – It turned into blood.
Moses told the Lord – "I'm not too smart you see
The Lord said, "Don't worry – You will speak through me."
All the men are dead – That sought to take your life
So go back to Egypt – Won't be so much strife.
Moses met with Aaron – And they both agreed
Aaron would do the talking – Explain all their needs.
They met with Pharoah – And Pharoah told them no
That he would not – Let their people go.
Pharoah said "Who is the Lord – Him I do not know
So I will not – Let your people go."
Pharoah was so angry – He was very mad
Over worked the people – Made them very sad.
Pharoah's heart was hardened – Said, "Give me a sign.
Show me a miracle – Then I might be fine."
So Moses took his rod – That was not a fake
Cast it on the ground – It turned into a snake.
Hit the river with the rod – all waters turned to blood
There's not water to drink – All of it was blood.
Pharoah's heart still hardened – Harder than a log
So, Aaron stretched out his rod – And sent a plague of frogs.
He agreed to free the people – If you remove the frogs right then
When Pharoah saw the frogs were gone – hardened his heart again.
So Aaron smote the dirt again – Became a plague of lice
Pharoah was so mad – He wasn't very nice
Then Moses charged him – sent a plague of flies
And just like before – He told them only lies.
The Lord said tell Pharoah – Let my people go
Or He would kill all their animals – Pharoah, now you know.
All of them died, - Just like he had said

But all the Israelite animals – Non of them was dead.
Take ashes from the furnace – Sprinkle shore to shore
When they fall on the people and beast – they'll be solid sores.
I'll send pestilence on them – all kinds of disease
Then their people will die – From all of these.
His heart is still hardened – tomorrow we will tell
I am sending on them – a big plgue of hail.
If you don't believe me – and protect yourself
I will kill everything – Won't be nothing left.
Pharoagh's had enough No more punishing me
Your God is real – This we all can see.
All Israelites left – And this is a fact
Only thing they had – was the clothes on their back.
After they had left – his heart hardened again
Said, Let's go chase them and capture all of them.
Got to the sea – said what will we do.
I'll open the water and you can pass on through
He opened up the sea – And it was dry land
They hurried on through – every woman and every man
The Israelites made it – They were on dry ground.
God released the water – Then Pharoah's army drowned.

Jesus is a Jealous God

Jesus is a jealous God – This we must confess.

His love is unmeasurable – For as the east is from the west.

Moses people did not obey – Seams they didn't care.

God put them in the wilderness – And left them forty years.

Prepare the way of the Lord - And make his path straight.

So his anger won't be kindled – and for you a bad fate.

Don't bow to graven images – For I am a jealous God.

And when it's time to judge - He will not spare the rod.

Jealousy is the rage of man – And it must be controlled.

If you plan to be with God – And walk those streets of Gold.

Love is a strong as death - And Jealousy like the grave.

So don't make God Jealous – and spoil the plans he made.

God is a real Jealous - will surely get revenge.

Don't tempt him in this area – cause he will surely win.

Jesus Is Crucified

Can you imagine how it hurt? – Thorns upon His head.
How very painful – I bet it really bleed.
Drove the nails in his hand – Probably parted bones.
God was surely watching – From high upon His throne.
He really loved us so – To die such a painful death.
Anytime He could have called – Angels there to help.
Then they went down – drove nails in His feet.
It hurt so very bad – Would not admit defeat.
Dropped the cross in the hole – I know it hurt him so.
The nails spread out the holes – where they had been drove.
All of this, He did for us. – Was because of His love.
While Father God was watching – From heaven up above.
Accept him as your savior – So all won't be in vain.
Everything He did for us – Enduring all that pain.
Ask Him to forgive your sins – And come into your heart.
He'll always be with you – And never more to part.

John the Baptist

Elizabeth was barren - but wanted a child.

Past her age to conceive - had waited a while.

An angel appeared to Zacharias - that day.

Said your prayer is answered - a baby on the way.

Elizabeth has conceived - she will have a son!

And the name - she shall give him - will be John.

God loosed his tongue - when he was a baby.

And he praised God - "That's what they say".

He preached baptism of repentance - for remission of sin.

In the country of Jordan - to those that heard him.

Some people though it - might have been funny.

His clothing carmel hair - food locust and honey.

Baptize me John - while on earth I live.

So all the scriptures - shall be fulfilled.

John said not worthy - to tie your shoe.

Jesus said John - "This is what you do."

When he was baptized - "Love came from above".

And lit on his shoulders - like the wings of a dove.

Wicked Herod - put John in jail

And was jealous of him - From the things he had said.

At Herod's birthday party - Herod's daughter came to dance.

Pleased Herod - said "Your wish I will grant."

What she wished for - was John the Baptist head.

The wish was granted - now John the Baptist is dead.

Jonah and the Whale

The Lord told Jonah – "Go to Nineveh, my son."
Jonah didn't want to – So what he did was run.
Jonah went to Joppa – There he found a ship.
There he boarded it – To Tarshish for his trip.
He hid down in the bottom – The sneaky little rat.
You don't hide from Jesus – He knows where you're at.
The Lord sent a mighty wind – The ship was bout to wreck.
All of them were very scared – The people on the deck.
They all cast lots - to find the evil one
The lot fell on Jonah – "It is you, my son."
The people asked Jonah – "What shall it be?"
Jonah said "Pick me up - and toss me in the sea."
They threw him in the sea – A big fish did prevail.
It swallowed him up – We think it was a whale.
This was the answer – It was God's will.
All of a sudden – It was peace be still.
He was in the fish's belly – Three days and nights.
Can you imagine – He was quite a sight.
This was so awful – He wished he was dead
With trash all around him – Weeds around his head.
You know God was with him – He is always there.
Jonah learned his lesson – He went to Him in prayer.
He went to Nineveh – There God's word he gave.
We are all hoping – That many there were saved.
Now you know the story – Hope you learned it well
This is the story – of Jonah and the whale.

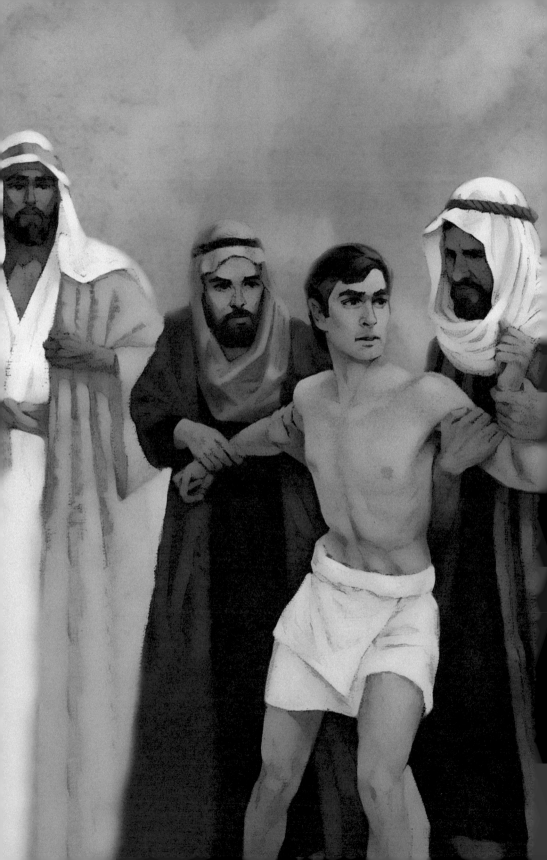

Joseph

Joseph was Jacobs' favorite son - made his brother rebellious.

Joseph was only seventeen - that's what the bible tells us.

Jacob made Joseph - a coat of many colors.

This made them more jealous - I'm talking about his brothers.

Joseph had a dream - his brothers would serve him.

When he told them - did not set well with them.

His father sent his brothers - to find the flock in Shechem.

Later he sent Joseph to check on them.

He could not find them - They had fled to Dothan.

They saw him coming said - "Let's kill the man".

Then they thought - "What will we tell our dad?"

If he thinks he's dead - he'll be very sad.

They saw him coming - stripped his coat of many colors.

Then threw him in a pit - I am talking about his brothers.

The pit was very deep - no water there within.

Then his brothers changed their minds again.

They sold him to the Israelites - as a slave.

Twenty pieces of silver was the price they paid.

Killed a kid goat and covered his coat in blood.

Sent it to his father - whom he really loved.

His father saw his coat - said this is surely his.

Was killed by a beast -That's the way it is.

His father told his family - I'll mourn for years and will never stop shedding tears.

Sold Joseph to *Potiphar. Pharoah's captain of the guard sent him to Egypt.*

He's in the hands of the Lord.

Pharoah had a dream, he could not understand.

Joseph revealed his dream, there'll be famine in the land.

55

Seven years of good, then seven years of bad.

Store up the good so you'll be ready for the bad.

Pharoah told his servants, there's no one in the land as smart as Joseph. He's surely God's plan. What Joseph had done, Pharoah thought was grand. So, he made Joseph ruler, throughout all his land. Made him in charge over all the rest.

Only one above him; was Pharoah himself.

Joseph planted crops throughout the land so he could store food.

This was his plan.

Warehouses full, there's corn everywhere. Ready for famine! Egypt won't even care.

Jacob, Josephs' father said, "We have no food – we must buy corn in Egypt. That's what we shall do."

He sent his sons to Egypt to buy corn for them to eat. When Joseph saw them coming , he thought that this is neat .

They had a brother named Benjamin, he was the youngest one.

Jacob kept him in Canaan. He was the youngest one.

They didn't recognize Joseph; he had changed quite a bit.

Since they sold him to slavery he was in the pit.

Joseph told them, you are spies sent out to our land to spy on us so you can make a plan.

They said, "no we are brothers and have the same dad.

Just ran out of food, this was very sad.

Put them in prison. For three days you see.

Then he came to them and said, "I'll set you free".

Take food to Jacob and bring Benjamin back to me.

I will keep him hostage, till I set you free.

Jacob was so sad to let Benjamin go.

Cause he lost Joseph, many years ago.

When they were returning home, they opened up a bag.

Money was in the top of it. Was this some sort of gag?

Opened up the other bags, money was in them.

Joseph had not charged a single cent to them.

The deal with Benjamin, almost made Jacob sick.

But, running out of food again. Had to do something quick.

They sent back the money.

Doubled the price.

Hoping Joseph would except it. Hoping he would be nice.

They brought Benjamin with them.

When they went there to buy; Joseph saw his brother and hid himself to cry.

Joseph told his brothers – you shall eat with me soon.

So they prepared a table for them to eat at noon.

He asked about their father, "tell me if you would," they said. They said he's alive and doing well. Really doing good.

His brothers did not know, that Joseph was their brother.

Thought he was Pharoahs man. Dealing one with the other.

Then, Joseph told them who he was. They were so afraid, afraid he would deal bad with them. Cause they sold him as a slave, Joseph was NOT angry.

It was in Gods plan.

To promote Joseph. To rule Egypt land.

After Pharoah heard of Josephs' family.

He said, "Go to Canaan and bring them to me. Bring all their possessions and all their money.

Bring them to the land; flowing with milk and honey."

Get a caravan of wagons.

Went to get his dad all his possessions. Everything he had.

Joseph was so happy, with all his family there.

God prepared everything; no pain left to bear.

Legion

This man was bound - with fettens and chains.

But, they would not hold him - he was insane.

He was in the mountains - cutting himself with stones.

The evil spirit in him - was mighty and strong.

When the Legion saw God said, "Please let me be - please dear Jesus. Don't torment me".

But, God had a plan - Evil spirit I'll bind.

I will cast you in - that heard of swine.

Cast them in the swine - and glory be.

The swine stampeded - into the sea.

They all drowned - and set the Legion free.

And the Legion was praising God - in his glory.

Lord, Help Me When I Fail

Make me not a stumbling block - Oh Father God, I pray.

Please fill me with your spirit - so they'll want to come my way.

Just let me be your shining light – So they'll see Christ in me.

Give me the words to say, Dear Lord - So they'll want to be set free.

I know I am unworthy - to witness for you Lord.

But please give me the courage - You said it'll not go void.

I know my life must seem a mess - when you look down on me.

But Lord, help me each step I take - for I am weak you see.

Lord, I love you very much - Please help me when I fail.

Just let me be a witness – If it keeps just one from hell.

I know if you could use me - to set one person free.

You might could find it in your heart - for a few more, don't You see?

I sure would hate to feel the pain - when you come back again.

To see someone I didn't tell - be it family or friend.

I can hear the screams and moans - as they're cast into hell.

"You should have told me about Jesus! - You have really failed.

Now they will spend eternity – In that dreadful heated place.

And now they will be cast away – No more to see God's face."

Please lift me up Dear God - and always let me tell,

About my loving Jesus – Lord, help me when I fail.

Love

Back in the early - days of our life,
Permission from the father - his daughter to wife.
Jacob talked to Laban - her father you see.
Said he wanted Rachel – His wife to be.
Then they agreed - He'd work seven years.
Then He could have Rachel - whom he loved so dear.
When the time was over - his plan really failed.
Her ugly sister Leah - was under the veil.
He worked seven more years - to have Rachel as his bride.
Although it wasn't his fault - that her father lied.
God was displeased with Laban - watching from above.
Blessed Jacob and Rachel - with His blessed love.

God loves people - by the thousands sent
Only thing He asks is - keep my commandments.
Love your neighbor as yourself - That is how its read.
Love the Lord thy God - with thy heart, soul and might.
Then He's always with you - whether day or night

Jonathan had more love - for Saul and Israel
Than any woman's love - that might prevail.
When the Lord loves you - it's not always just fun.
He will correct you - like the father does his son.
I love them - and they love me.
Those that seek - shall find me.
Hatred stirs strife - Love covers sin.
Keep Jesus in your heart - You will surely win.
Those that love - knowledge and hate reproof,

Keep your minds open - and you will learn the truth.
A friend loveth - all the time.
But a brother loveth - when its fine.
Don't sleep too much - Love more.
Or poverty - may knocks on your door.

A time for love - a time for hate.
A time for peace - war can wait.
Hate the evil - love the good
Keeps you happy - at least, it should.
Don't imagine evil against your neighbor.
Stay his friend and keep him stable.
Love your enemies to the end.
Pray for them - they'll be your friend.
Can't love God and Mammon - Love one or the other.
Hope you choose God - No mistake there brother.
Love your neighbor as yourself - Then all should be well.
Love your neighbor as yourself - Help keep you out of hell.
We have iniquity hanging around - It is surely old.
And the love of money - may even wax you cold.
Love you're enemy as yourself - That is what you do.
Put a smile on Jesus' face - He'll take care of you.
For God so loved the world - gave His only son.
That whosoever believeth in Him -in heaven will have fun.
If you love one another - you'll be God's disciple.
Keep your love together - and be sure not to triffle.
Giving your life for your friend –
Is awesome, don't you see? - Jesus died upon the cross - Did the same for you and me.
Let love be pure - If only you would
And cleave to that - which is only good.

God love a cheerful giver - so give from your heart.

God thanks you so much - for giving Him His part.

We all need - to serve each other with love.

And God will surely bless you - from heaven up above.

God loved us so much - Gave His life on the cross.

Then If we accept him - we will not be lost.

Husband love your wife - What he wants you to do.

Wife love your husband - so both of you are true.

Love of money is the root of all evil - but money itself is not.

So please don't worship it - Just take care of what you got.

Young women love your husband - and your children too.

So when they grow up - they'll know what to do.

Make Room for Jesus

In the town of Bethlehem - Was where Jesus Christ was born.
With no room in the inn – His birthplace was a barn.
She wrapped Him in swaddling clothes – And laid Him in a manger.
The animals knew about Him – So there wasn't any danger.
The shepherds were tending their flocks – Even though it was at night.
The angel of the Lord came – In a beautiful shinning light.
The shepherds there were sore afraid – Is this birth a normal boy?
The angel said, "Be not afraid - I bring tidings of great joy.
For unto you is born this day - our savior Jesus Christ."
Just believe and put your trust in Him – You'll have eternal life.

He's in the manger in swaddling clothes – So down the trail they trod
While the multitude of heavenly hosts – Were singing praises unto God.
Jesus was walking here on earth – Over thirty years.
Preaching, teaching, healing – Wanted all to see and hear.
We'll make many decisions – Throughout all our lives.
Accept Him as your savior – And receive eternal life.
Right where you are, bow you head. – Ask Jesus to come in.
Ask Him to forgive you, - And you want to live for Him.
There He'll save you from your sins. – And claim you as his own.
You'll be His child forever more, - And share His glorious throne.

Money and Faith

I'll tell you something - that might seem funny.

Look what God did - without money.

Created heavens and earth - Money will have to wait.

Created all of this - strictly on his faith.

With God watching from above - Money will have to wait.

Everything going on - is strictly done by faith.

Devil fought Goliath - on that fatal date.

And he killed him - because of his faith.

God goes to heaven - to prepare us a place.

The way we claim it - is only through our faith.

God sent Moses - to that Egypt land.

To be free of Israelite's - from ole Pharaoh's land.

Moses was worried - what will be my fate.

God said - Don't worry - Just have a little faith.

God fed five thousand - this is what is said.

With two little fishes - and five loaves of bread.

You see friend money - is NOT what's so great.

God don't need your money - he just needs your faith.

Natural and Spiritual Body

Natural and Spiritual Bodies – Is how you are formed.

One of them is lust – The other could be harm.

The choice belongs to you – Which one will you choose.

Will you choose the bad one? – If so you probably loose.

The lady on the corner – Would it be very hard?

To look at her in lust – or tell her about the Lord.

Then there's the sick – And he's so in despair.

Would you try to help – Or would you even care?

Cashier gave you too much change – when you paid the bill.

Would you want to keep it – So your pockets you could fill?

The driver on the freeway – trying to crowd in

Do you want to cuss him out – Or say, "Go ahead my friend."

Natural Spiritual you have been shown. Which road will you trod?

Lustful one for you – Or spiritual one for God?

When you're being judged – And don't know what to do,

You certainly don't want Him to say –" Depart I never knew you."

So prepare yourself and be ready – When that moment comes

So God will say "I Love You. Come on in my son."

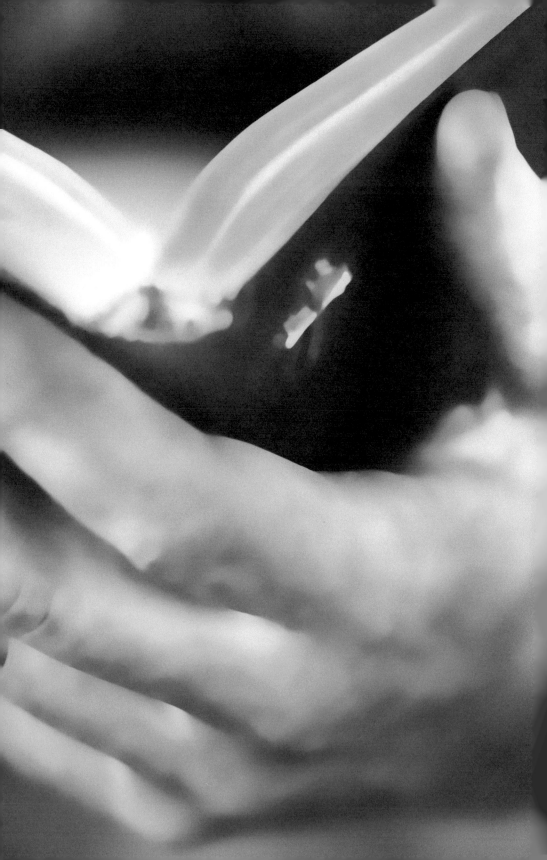

No Excuse

I wrote all these poems- Especially for you!

To share Jesus with you- Tell you what to do.

Jesus is a loving God- Far as the East is from the West.

But, you have to accept him-To pass this test.

Believe he died on the cross- To forgive our sins.

You open upon your hearts' door-Let Jesus come in.

When he comes again- You will go to hell.

Each poem that I have written- Has a meaning for you.

Read them very carefully-You'll know what to do.

We know not the day or hour-When he'll come back again.

Prepare yourself now-So, you'll be ready my friend.

No in between- The decision you have to make.

Hope you do it soon-Before, it's too late.

If you wait too long-Won't be any use.

It will be too late-Won't be an excuse.

No Other Gods Before Me

No other Gods before me - that is how its read.
No other Gods before me - that is what he said.
No other images before me - whether land or sea.
I am a jealous God - so only worship me.
Do not take my name in vain - that would make me mad.
The consequences you will receive - will be very bad.
Remember the Sabbath keep it Holy - That should be the best.
All we do on this day - is get plenty of rest.
Honor mom and dad - This is what you do.
To pay back some of the things - that they did for you.
You shall NOT kill - These words came from him.
Their life don't belong to you - it belongs to them.
Do NOT commit adultery - listen to me sir.
She don't belong to you - Till you marry her.
Thou shall not steal - It belongs to someone else.
Don't be greedy – and take it for yourself.
Don't tell a lie - It is so uncouth.
What you are doing- Is stealing the truth.
Don't covet the neighbors house - Or his wife inside.
She belongs to him – And with him should abide.

Noah

God was unhappy - His world was full of sin.

Said He'd destroy it - and start over again.

He sent the rains - forty days and nights.

That should do it – Not a bit of earth in sight.

God saw grace in Noah - and his family.

Said - I want you - to build an ark for me.

Noah had three sons, each of them had wives.

That made eight - to start the new life.

Ark shall be four-fifty long - and seventy-five wide.

Forty-five feet tall - and three stories high.

The ark to be made of gopher wood - Pitch every side.

So, it would be sealed - no leaks inside.

Everything of flesh - shall be taken, two by two.

Into the ark - so they can be with you.

Cattle, beast or fowls - I'll tell you why.

Must be male and female - so they can multiply.

Noah did exactly - what God told him to do.

Then all of God's plans - would be carried through.

Of the clean you will take seven - of the unclean take two.

Each with its mate – This is what you do.

God sent the rains - forty days and nights.

The Ark was sturdy - Everything was all right.

The water was there - a hundred fifty days.

The it receded - Everything was OK.

All left the Ark - stepped out on the earth.

That was the beginning - of replenishing the earth.

Old Thoughts

I used to think that I was having fun - with all the things I'd do.

But, that was just before - I started serving you.

I'd go out dancing, drinking - carousing with the girls.

Only thing, I was looking for - was pleasures of the world.

That's nothing compared to Jesus - nothing can't you see.

Nothing compared to Jesus - and his blessed loved for me.

Now I'm serving Jesus - he gave me a break.

Each morning when I wake up - watch each step I take.

For I'm just a person - that's been saved by grace.

And I need your constant prayer - as each day I face.

Chapter Sixteen of Isaiah - verses Nineteen is the one.

I'm not gonna need the moon - on light of the sun.

For I have the blessed father - who watches day and night.

With his love and mercy - is my everlasting light.

Some people, I might have led astray - Let me tell you what to do.

Just put your trust in Jesus - he will see you through.

He's there when you need him - not like some friend that's gone.

All you do is call on him - you don't even need a phone.

Paul

Saul made havoc – of the church.

In God's eyes- he was a jerk.

He captured men - and women too.

Put them in prison - That's what he's do.

He was mean to Christians - we know well.

Would take them to prison - put them in jail.

He journeyed to Damascus -This we agree.

A bright light shone on him - He could not see.

He fell to the earth - Heard a voice say.

"Saul, why do you - persecute me today?"

Saul said – Lord - is that you?

"Yes, this is Jesus - Here's what you do."

Saul was trembling - didn't know what to do.

The Lord said - "Here's what you do.

Go to the city - they will tell you."

Saul went to the city - could hardly think.

For three days - did not eat or drink!

Ananias was there - and he did wait.

For Saul at the street -they called Straight.

He put his hands on him - He received his sight.

Scales fell off - everything was all right.

Saul was baptized - This is what you do.

Now he is preaching - to me and to you.

Jesus changed his name - it's no more Saul.

Jesus changed it - Now his name is Paul.

Plant That Precious Seed

That corn that you are eating - at one time was a seed.

And then it was planted - so your family it would feed.

At first there was nothing -Then the sprout begins to grow,

And multiplies to millions – As you're looking down each row.

When you tell someone of Jesus - you're planting that precious seed.

Then God will give the increase as He shall see the need.

Your labor is not in vain - when you speak of God - you see.

Through praying and believing - then all of it shall be.

When someone hears of Jesus - the foundation is laid.

But it may not show an increase - for many many days.

The switch that turns the light on - and changes the night to day.

Just be a switch for Jesus - and show someone the way.

Don't hide your light of Jesus - Let everybody know.

Accept Him as their savior - and walk those streets of gold.

He died there upon the cross - to supply or every need.

Just tell everyone of Jesus - and plant that precious seed.

Playing With Your Phone

Dust on the Bible - It's setting there alone.

Nobody's reading it -They're playing with their phone.

Sharing someone with Jesus - preparing them for the throne.

Said, "I'm busy now - I'm playing with my phone."

Jesus died on the cross - preparing our heavenly home.

We didn't pay attention - We were playing with our phone.

When He come back again - There be screaming and moans.

We did not accept Him - We were playing with our phone.

I heard the trumpet sound - He's come to claim his own.

You will be in hell - for playing with your phone.

Just before this happens – Get in a difference zone.

Accept Him as your Savior - Quit playing with your phone!

Ruth

Naomi was Ruth's Mother-in-law - whom she loved so dear.

After her husband died - wanted to keep her near.

Naomi told Ruth -"Go on your way."

Ruth said "No"- With Naomi she would stay.

They left Moab - Bethlehem did appeal.

So, they went there - Ruth worked in the field.

She worked for Boaz - a wealthy man.

Cleaned corn and barley - throughout his land.

Then Boaz noticed her - She leaves her mark.

She walked in the fields - from daylight to dark.

He had compassion for her - Said to his fellows,

"Leave extra for her - easy for her to gather."

Naomi was proud of her - with all she did do.

And she told her - "The Lord is blessing you."

Boaz had eaten, drank - was going to sleep

When Ruth came to him - and laid at his feet.

He woke at midnight and - was very scared.

Looked at her and said - "Who is laying there?"

She said - "It's Ruth" - Now it is known.

Was the most kindness - that had ever been shown.

He went through all kinsmen - to protect his pride.

So he could make Ruth -his precious bride.

The Devil's Hurting You!

The devil's always hurting you - He is so very mean.

Anytime there's trouble - he's always on the scene.

You don't have to take it - See what the Bible tells.

Pray about it, brother - Leave Satan there is hell.

It may be alcohol that rules you all the time.

Or, it may be cigarettes that surely rules your mind.

Maybe its some kind of dope - Could it be cocaine,

That has you in its power - and burning up your brain?

You may have a sickness - that Satan put on you.

God can surely heal it - Just read your Bible through.

It tells you of the power that you can have - you see.

Just cast those demons out - and make old Satan flee.

Maybe its your love one that he has lead astray.

The way to cure the problem - Get on your knees and pray.

Don't let Satan beat you - Study God's word.

Then you can be a winner - and beat that dirty bird.

The devil walks to and fro - He's surely everywhere.

He doesn't have a pitchfork - or long red underwear.

He'll paint your mind a picture that looks so good - you see.

He'll come up on your blind side - Both to you and me.

The Door

Compare your heart like it is a door - No doorknob outside.

Only way to open it – Is by you from the inside.

Means you are the only way – For someone to come in

So when God knocks on the door – Will you let Him in?

We know your heart is full of sin – Also filled with strife

Accept Him as your savior – And receive eternal life.

Confess with your mouth - and believe in your heart.

That God raised Him from the dead – you want him in your heart.

For with the heart, man believes – with the mouth confessions made

Accept Him as your Savior – And be saved today

He died upon the cross – Just for you and me.

It cost you nothing – cause your salvation is free.

Thank you so much, Jesus – for providing us a way,

For us to go to heaven – And with you always stay.

The Eternal Decision

There is a hereafter! - What will it be?
Heaven or Hell? - Up to you and me.
We have a decision - that we have to make.
Will you choose Hell - Or God's pearly gates?
The Bible tells us - we have all sinned.
Must open our hearts door - and let Jesus come in.
He died on the cross - for me and for you.
Just ask him to save you -That's all that you do.
He went on to heaven - to prepare us a place.
If we would proclaim - His saving grace.
He's building us mansions - streets paved with gold.
You have no excuse now - for you have been told.
So bow your head - Let Jesus come in.
He'll be your savior - your Lord, and your friend.
He'll always be with you - wherever you go.
I'll see you, my friend - on those streets of gold.
There's another choice - where you may go.
It's called Hell -way down below.
Where, the fire never ceases - and the worm dieth not.
The pain so severe - and your body so hot!
You'll want another chance - but there is no way.
You made your decision - in Hell you will stay.
So I'll ask you again - before its too late.
Choose my dear Jesus - and don't have that fate.

The Little Man

Zacchaeus was a little man – Very, very small.
When Jesus passed through the crowd -couldn't see Him at all.
So, Zacchaeus must figure out – What could he do?
So, he could see Jesus - when he passed through.

He looked down the road - and saw a sycamore tree.
"I'll climb up in it - Then I can see."
Jesus passed by - Said, "I'll tell you what to do.
Come down out of that tree - I'm going home with you."

So, Zacchaeus no more felt - that he was small.
He felt like he was - ten feet tall.
Zacchaeus was very rich - He gave it all to the poor.
Now he walks the streets of Gold on Gods celestial shore.

The Parodical Son

There was a certain man - that had these two sons.

The older one was smart - The younger one was dumb.

The young was high spirited – Wanting to have fun.

"Give me my inheritance - I'll take it and I'll run."

In riotous living, he wasted it - Soon it was gone!

Thinking of his father - and the things back home.

He got a job in the fields - feeding swine.

Didn't have any food - so with the swine did dine.

Eating corn with the swine – "I don't know what to do."

Disappointed in himself - "I'll try to think it through.

My father's hired servants - have plenty to eat.

I have sinned against the Lord - I feel so incomplete.

I'll go back home and ask my Dad - if I can work for him."

When he saw me coming – I surely had been missed.

He ran and greeted me - with kiss - after kiss.

Bring the best robe - I want it to look neat.

Put a ring on his finger and shoes upon his feet.

Bring forth the fatted calf -We will kill and eat.

My son is back home - It is a special treat.

His son was like a sheep - that had gone astray.

Was welcomed him back again - We'll celebrate this day.

Compare us to this son - What would God say to us?

Would He forgive us? Or would he raise a little fuss?

He would say - "Forgiven - go and sin so more.

Welcome back my son - I'll open heaven's door.

The "Sauce"

That old beer and alcohol – Is what I call the "Sauce."
Sooner or later – It will surely be a loss.
May be one of your loved ones – Or maybe just a friend
Or someone that's been shopping – Their life you might end.

While driving down the highway – Saw that awful crash
This two-year-old baby – I knew she couldn't last
She died in my arms – She had paid the cost.
For the mother that was driving – Had been on the "Sauce."

I was visiting some friends – When I heard a scream
I ran to see what happened – It seemed like a dream
Her husband had been beating her – Said "I'll show you who's Boss.
I'll drink when I want to – Because I love my "Sauce."

Children are rejected – And sometimes are abused
When there's Alcohol around – Whose gonna pay the dues?
Those dear little children – Let me tell you, dude.
The sauce took all their money – And there is no food.

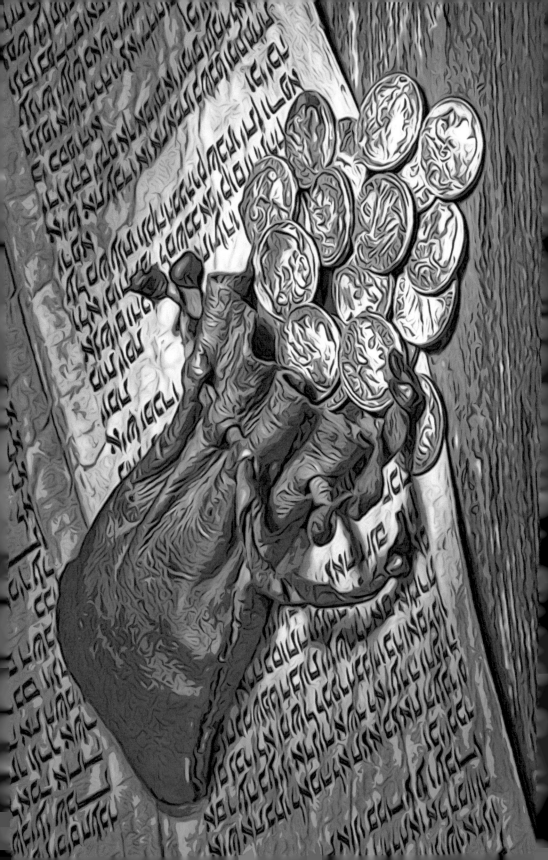

Thirty Pieces of Silver

Thirty pieces of silver - Judas was paid.

To betray Jesus - on that fatal day.

Judas asked the priest - What'll you give me,

To point out Jesus - So Him you can see?

When you're in the crowd - you cannot miss.

He is the one - that I will kiss.

They laid hands on Him - and took him away.

Thirty pieces of silver - was the price that was paid.

Friend, let me ask you - What would you ask?

To point out Jesus - and destroy your past.

Would it be a woman - that leads you on?

Destroy your hopes - of your heavenly home?

Or could it be - alcohol or dope.

That you would trade - for your heavenly hope?

Don't be like Judas - with all of his greed.

Put your trust in Jesus - He'll supply your need.

Two Little Fishes and Five Loaves of Bread

Five thousand people - listening to Jesus speak,
All of them were hungry - with nothing to eat.
People were upset - they didn't know what to do.
It would take a lot of money - to buy all the food.
One little lad was there - here is what he said,
"I've got two little fishes - and five loaves of bread."
Get in groups of fifty - and here is what you do.
Then I will bless it - and God will feed you.
All of them ate - and it sure was good!
What they had left - was twelve baskets full.
Can you imagine - Five thousand fed!
With two little fishes - and five loaves of bread.

Watching You

Jesus don't need a plane - he don't need a car.

He always knows exactly - where you are.

So always be careful - everything you do.

Because Jesus - is always watching you.

He watches you, while you sleep - or when you are awake.

So, you need to be careful - for heaven's sake.

He's all over the world - in the bottom of the sea.

He's constantly busy - watching you and me.

I know he gets upset - some of the things we do.

We keep him really busy - watching me and you.

Before you commit that sin - here's what you do.

Don't do it, you know he's watching you.

Let's make Jesus proud - here's what we do.

Don't be bad - you know he's watching you.

Where The Fire Will Never Cease

That gas truck that was burning – One the road today
It was so dreadfully hot – That I stayed far, away.
I hope whoever was in it – Made their hasty escape
Because if they didn't – It would surely be too late.

And then I thought of Jesus – When he comes back again
There will be no escape – It will surely be your end.
If you have not accepted him – You'll weep and gnash your teeth
Where the worm dieth not – And the fire will never cease.

That chemical plant was burning – And there was no control
The flames were shooting in the sky – In a fiery fiery gold.
I don't know what started it – and did everybody flee?
Cause the heat was so unbearable – Many thousand degrees

And then I thought of Jesus – When he comes back again
There will be no escape – It will surely be your end.
If you have not accepted him – You'll weep and gnash your teeth
Where the worm dieth not, oh Lord – And the fire will never cease.

The atomic bomb that was dropped – in that foreign land
Was really devastating – Destruction was as planned.
There (were) many, many people killed – yet some did get away
And lived to tell the story – To their grandkids today.
And then I thought of Jesus – When he comes back again
There will be no escape – It will surely be your end.
If you have not accepted him – You'll weep and gnash your teeth
Where the worm dieth not, oh Lord – And the fire will never cease.

Where Two or More Are Gathered

Except Jesus as your Savior - before he comes back again.

When he appears in the clouds - It will be too late my friend.

The verdict is all really made - hope you chose it well.

You either going to heaven - or you will be in hell.

Two people working in the field -then one of them is gone.

The one left will be in hell -the other at God's Throne.

Two of you are there in bed - then your partners gone.

She went on to heaven - left you there alone.

You are driving down the road - then your partner left.

He is now in heaven - left you by yourself.

You are there in college - Classmates everywhere.

Then they disappear - left you sitting there.

God don't want this to happen - He don't want you alone.

Ask him to come in your heart - and all meet at the throne.

You Can Beat the Devil

Sickness and diseases are spread throughout all our land,
But that don't (doesn't) mean the end my friend. There's (There is) another
plan.
Belief and dedication – I don't mean playing games
Then you can beat the Devil – If you Pray in Jesus's name
You may have some love ones – That's headed straight to hell
But don't give up on them – Here's a way that you won't fail
Belief and dedication – And I don't mean playing games.
Then you can beat the Devil – If you pray in Jesus's name
Your marriage may be shaky – And headed for the Rocks
Just listen to me friend – It's time for that to STOP.
Belief and dedication – And I don't mean playing games.
Then you can beat the Devil – If you pray in Jesus's name
Habits and addictions – are sometimes hard to break
Think of the ones around you – And how you make them ache
Belief and dedication – And I don't mean playing games.
Then you can beat the Devil – If you pray in Jesus's name
Our kids are growing up now – Out in this world of sin
The devil's always after them – But we don't want him to win.
Belief and dedication – And I don't mean playing games.
Then you can beat the Devil – If you pray in Jesus's name

Your Daddy Loves You So

I must have been mixed up – A long, long time ago.

Why I left my babies – I will never know.

Please Kim and Jas forgive me – I miss you, so you see.

When I signed those papers – Must have been insanity.

We met down at the courthouse – And took my rights away.

Except for visitation – I'll never forget that day.

Partings are so awful - and this we all know.

Please Kim and Jas forgive me – Your daddy loves you so.

I'm a long, long way from you – And the pain is so severe.

I miss you so, my babies – And I long to have you near.

I think of you each day – And I dream of you at night.

I really messed things up – Wish that I'd done right.

Today you'll see me smiling – 'Cause I am on my way

To see my Kim and Jason – It's visitation day.

But the time will pass so fast – Then I'll have to go.

Please Kim and Jas forgive me – Your daddy loves you so.

THE END